DIFFERENT DARKNESSES

Different Darknesses

Jason Morris

fmsbw

San Francisco, California

ISBN-10 1-7329439-2-3
ISBN-13: 978-1-7329439-2-6

"Another Green World" owes its title directly to the painting by Nicole Eisenman, which is taken from the Brian Eno record.

"An Exchange" is derived from Chuang Tzu's "Seeing Things as Equal," and relies on Burton Watson's translation of the inner chapters.

Versions of some of these poems originally appeared in *HIGH NOON*, *spoKe*, and *Elderly*.

Cover artwork by Terry St. John
Cover photo by Kevin Miller
Author photo by Sally Morris

fmsbw
San Francisco, California

For Sally

CONTENTS

DIFFERENT DARKNESSES

Only suffering makes sense—
why you return to it so. As what

meaning's made of, out
from where it comes. & so

you approach it every which way
bellowing on all fours, like a bull

Asleep on your side in the moonlight
suffering comes after you in dreams

& walking the sand on the sunlit hazy
coast. You come after it stuttering

joyful, only half making sense
(since you barely half feel it, can't

see it) in different darknesses.
In kindness you approach pain holding

flowers, tracking mud & dirt on
your arrival at the white plaster

house at the edge of the desert.
They are playing marimbas, there are

roughly woven red blankets on
the floor. You engrave your refrains

on stone slabs, hurl them into the dunes
of hot sparkling sand. In hours of sun-

light you rehearse your approach, each of
the movements you'll make—toward pain

& away from it: carefully charted
noiseless, studied, deliberate—

made in accord with your most ancient feeling
an endless attraction to something with no name

ANOTHER GREEN WORLD

You come seesawing into being
somehow sidelong, as she
stares at the back cover, the
young musician in monochrome
green beside the potted flowers—
a list of worlds, names of
songs. Nighttime's what this
space is in, mutely expands
into—every word swells out,
a part of and underneath
the conversation. The left plane
practically vertical, slides
down forcefully to the side of
the big orange feet splayed under
a variously aligned table
at a party at a friend's apartment
that turned into eternity, or
became the whole universe
in the form of several sprawling
and intimate rooms. Closely
conjoined, containing all colors
variously buzzed and dreaming
a record of many nights in an
instant as he looked down into
his phone. And under the slowly
wheeling little silver lights
of the disco ball over towards
the bedroom, the two friends drink
beer and talk. Off by the exit
of the balcony, taking over from
the fading day you look out
at the East River and the white

lights of the skyline, watch them
reflected rendered in quick
notation of fats to leans or in
gorgeous detail. Aside from being
one of my favorite doors left ajar
this is also a song at points of
time giving you the impression
something definite has ended:
I knew it was also another
green world right away. I saw it
in her hands from the other
side of the room "You'd be
surprised / at my degree of
uncertainty." Saw it from across
the gallery. Rauch means smoke
in German—new smoke in naked
embrace, with strong blue arms
orange and cubist, blowing
rings up at the ceiling and your
lean black hands hold the black disc
sideways over the little turntable. She
had just blown a couple lines beside
you, felt that sharply pleasant pain
and drip in her red right nostril. And
having just arrived—drunkenly
surveying the scene, saying hello
in pinkish fats like a Bacon or Guston
you were welcomed, sweet slow dance
in the center of the room
forever held together at
the threshold, in the half-light:
a pack of Newports, the figure in
paint thinner slices different types
of meats and cheeses by two bottles

of red and a delicate sprig
of something bright pink, a
rose. Across the table, he lights
a joint for the guy in the Nets hat, his
handsome face briefly and suddenly
will now always be illuminated blue
over bright knit plaid collar. It echoes
the blue August moon
the blue of the room
its concentric circles and shaded cubes
recall Edvard Munch, the Old
Masters. Grace Jones on the Alicia
McCarthy-looking carpet. And behind
the sofa the couple's hands form
a perfect knot, a circle equally
floating, holding a strong position
the long duration of momentary love
on a small blue and red field. A
flag. There are three half empty
Coronas and a rolled up ten, you are
about to pass out in the arms of your
boyfriend or girlfriend, your best
friend—beautifully buzzed and sharing
a practically impossible permeable
border with everyone, an edge that isn't
really an edge. Androgynous at the
periphery of one particular night
sexy but just getting started or even
winding to a close in the pause
each figure partakes of. The three
friends are still outside, talking, smoking
in the cool night air you can almost
feel it, they are outside on the balcony
they look out over the river forever

LINES

First grids
then stripes
Backbone then jaw
then lungs, as
what once was
Solar nebula
spun out to form
our ancestors in
an explosion of stars.

"Yeah, but a minute
is quite a while,"
said Agnes Martin
about looking at
paintings she made.

Meteorites
& other small old
relics—teeth,
bone. The mind's
feel for time, its home

a hand smoothing
felt. Striped light
remembered in
wide murmurs of
rays disappearing
Canadian prairie

evening sun seem-
ing woven into its
wave function collapse
hovering on what
seems like but is
too big to be sky

& dies there in a
flash. To breathe
life into something
means it must be
bound to become
a corpse, decay

its armature
quick now, held
just perceptibly
in pencil under, as
a hum or a prayer—
awareness, slowly
expanding there

STAY LIVE

It takes bravery
& the exacting placement
Knowing when & where to dig
like even here
Flight VX 0926
with service to Los Angeles
Reading the great unruly & utterly sane
Good Doctor's translation
of "The Man Who Resembled a Horse"
Free for the taking
This healthy decomposing soil
even amid the sterile, zonked out
no-places of airport, airplane
"we've been in this water so long
we don't even notice it's boiling"
Here is somewhere to stand
& to dig: I am a poet of the future
a root encountering a decomposing corpse
following a lead
Seat 19 F
my brain is about
to follow the curvature
of the California coast
through the bright gray patches
of fog that still cling to it
Look out over my right shoulder
going along toward you & the very
Pacific you know. Later,
these sessile thoughts will
inhabit a quiet room
swell at their little green stems
& so turn brittle & fall
into words. How I wish
I could tell you

how total at times
is my love for you. Like
catching sight of
a mountain on hazy
horizon. Something
suddenly seen clearly
that was never not there

NIGHT

Automated food robots

PTSD, organ failure

w/ sunny smile

in digital delivery

GMO corn food past

soon to be underwater

public transit center

we go to when we go places

restaurants parties shows

even as simple as

Him having lost it

guy on the bus

gone, screaming

Like being in a video game

O well I guess I did that

too. Automate

stop. Think of who you

live with. Chill

the fuck out. They

do that too from time to

time you know (think

of you). See

what you are looking at

Engaging the teeth

of the gear

of the appetite

Desire finds

finite form

edging the void

fleshy in subsets

filthy tired skin

set against its metal teeth

to let it turn & turn

the night stays elegant

almost in miniature

musical accompaniment

lighted doorways, just so.

There is nothing to say however

about the sky

Same old familiar sky it was

since childhood

Take traction—go

in what you are

afraid of, love most fully

Grubs & beetles, worms

The sun going down

in shifts of revenant

remnant light

The weight that pulls

words down

for shared use

that they might make us

by making momentary

use of us, & so

deliver us both

FORTUNE

Begun in the middle
A familiar story
left off half told
a man trying to see
his way home to
his wife. Gone
astray. Shipwreck,
misery & evil: "He
ended it, and no one
moved," is how the
center of the story
begins. Under big
silver skies
witchcraft & pollution
the audience sits in a
darkening hall. To
arrive at some kind of
afterlife, a city
familiar & shining—
You enter in disguise
pause to make sure
the words are
correct, align
just trying to get
home. The afterlife
of words, what
a poem is. Repair

   home, re-

      pair

SPOON

Now fully night, but
soft—palm trees over
painted refineries
waxing, tall unleaded light
A gas station, that rock
at the perimeter getting
full, seems close. Casual learning
someone you sort of knew, who
died, was briefly homeless.
A shock. All that would have
interested him about this train
or the sentence you use
to describe it is grammar,
getting some rest on the far
back seat. Wait—remain
underground on the platform
able to give anyone directions
anywhere. A smoothness
almost tastable, blood or
copper, the rocking of steel
tracks and wheels.
Something deliberate,
motion along a line
seen in the mind's eye
even as words & windows
darken & blur, racing by

22 VIII 18

104%
for John Coletti

Isn't it always there, the residue

concern leaves

        Whose power's perceived as

a weakness   Pure benevolence

Sunlit second story, shades by keys

& water, reading   in order to wrest from

the difficulty of writing   form, some

similar retreat

Different facet of the same stone. See how

as it's turned

        Windowsills, chipped paint. Old

& the panes themselves sure, clear of

awareness. Unexcelled awareness of windows

That some new sensation is certain to follow—

is already with you

        Or do you occasionally feel

the present form is final

        15 VII 19

16

OTHER HOUSE

Piblokto
in the West Oakland
dive, mid-summer
hysteria (PiL—
Low Life, plus
all spring's agony)
might make one
murderous, or
jog naked thru
night time air
tripping on acid in
the smell of jasmine
the neighborhood
nearby this one in
memory. Nearly two
decades ago. Yelling
on swing sets thirty
blocks later rolling
down Broadway. The
elements insist you're in
someone else's house
again. Same brain
you were born
with, a memory
For a moment one thing
you can agree with
your younger self on—
water still takes
the shape of waves
offshore. Blackly
curling. Customary
within anything
seemingly self-identical:

amplitude / decrease.

Distinguished
Extinguished
No no
All the way neither

JOB

The senses
are what
The world
returns to, not
you. You if
you're even
microbes, or
oxygenated
A specific
coral color
blue rust green
fiery orange

Eat. In liquid
darknesses
widening
so as to make
any periphery
sensed visible

Night-time city
as searchlight
or campfire

Appetite
how lichen forms
in broad daylight
Even machines get
unsettled it seems
start going
for no
what's called

reason. How
weightlessly

one drops
as a mind
is a body, or

only ever is
embodied

& so always
gets going
on actual
premises:

corners
of streets
or on
the side of

a rock—
taking stock
of real
surroundings
is initial
therefore
perpetual job

TEMPLES

These temples

of the benthos

pure rain, castles

of the profane

imagination.

You're gone

for days, & on

reappearance

can't say where

you've been.

Muddy foot tracks.

I like that I said

I think

at the end of

that sentence

If I do right by

them it doesn't

matter, I'll be

doing alright

by everyone

I think. But

I try & not

wrack my brains

anymore—easy

answers

& flowers are just

as suddenly so

lost,

same old

questions to try

to work through

but different

& through all

the necessary

complications.

Combinations.

Mind's only real

survival tactic is

it can't exist

at present. Just

in deixis

In drive &

reverse: it was

there then

later on

will be. Well

it was & does

Odd

postal formats

it recognizes

itself in what

shouldn't be

here. What is it

summer hours

parking garage

tying off

the vein

preparing

the dose

lazily spiking

Some higher use

a body gets

put to—not sex

or work, sacred

though as

either is but

more tangential

graves, wildflowers

Religion but not so

stopgap. One

eternity a single

presence

can't include

fail to solve & still

clearly show

the work

In fact resolve

to fail

TAKE

seeing white

& brown

mottled

pigeon

Of sludge

under

luxury tower

Amenities

urban struggle

in reflection

of leaves on

windshield,

silver

sedan

Momentarily

passing

one-hitter at

stoplight,

tapping out

ash

Mid-market

construction

everyone imagines

their meal-ticket is

Not exhausting

the conditional

The rage

that peace

comes out of

LIGHT

Getting rid
of discomfort
is a dance move
& shows the very
notions of
scarcity / abundance
even pain to be

fictive—
pure result
of crooked human
looking. Qualities
not present
in nature, only there
misperception
brought late to the game
ugly sideways glances
at what light simply
illuminates.

Numinous therefore
sacred as such.
Likewise cause
& effect are
identical, when
clearly viewed.
To watch what
you do as you go

& see how many
of your dances
were done on

ordinary days
ordinary light,
made of routine
hours, displaying
shape posture
& movement therein—
present as they go

LAPSE

Soft, like
something actual
were waiting,
a material
maybe
waiting / writing
sifting a thought
that, yeah
a what not
Of wanting

test results
back, my blood
in the hospital
it's information. I'm full
of it. First it's food

& what nourishes me
initially unlike me
becomes me
That activity of it
turning into it, what
I know or am
the Greeks called
psyche

This ancient
sense of soul
as something
taking place
between
two lapses

one emptiness
and another

beside myself
some books
silently piled

Bells in situ

A window
left open
at night

to let
love in. Mind
is always effective
cause. Nothing
ever pauses

calls out in
passing, and it
responds.
Brake lights
out the rainy
window signal

night came on.
Is there some
simpler way of
reading my blood

AN EXCHANGE

Sitting with his back against the wall, breathing heavy & staring at the sky, as though he'd lost a friend, his wife, or his mind, your companion tells you, "You're not the same as yourself." After a kind of extended, crazy pause, he goes on, "But high up in the woods, where it's windy and wet—mist cool in the branches—there is a whole lot of tearing, breaking & rumbling going on, all the time. Fluttering leaves in the breeze, groaning trees, constant noise. Down here on earth, in cities, people play music, guitars, pianos. Nothing difficult, just whistling & blowing, human practice. After awhile, counterpoint, melody, & so forth emerge."

So you consider this, while your friend remains seated, now in silence, his back still against the brick wall. The loud sounds of breakage, groaning tree limbs, wind and rain in high places is conjoined in your mind with the music people in cities make. And in that merging there is for you the momentary but forceful (because formal) severance of the old notion of some death-like Other, which for years you'd held in mind. Cradled, insisted upon. Instead you now begin to picture how a spider might go about ordering its web. And so you start to recognize yourself in a world made by others, insistent (as they must of necessity have been) on the forms that made themselves visible.

BLEACH

Enough
w/ the self-
consideration
Every angle
cheapest stuff you got
fully absorbed yet
Nothing
but trouble
blinking ordinary
darkened amusements
Then again
late afternoon light
Capacity
it makes of the mind
just to open, look & see
how much doubt
can be levitated
& spell in different voices
Paying even attention
Stutter
to what attention is given
permission to fall away
in sidewalk grackle
bass on love buzz
the very permanent
wandering
specific to
a lostness
looseness
that gravity granted you, grace
Work yr way into
pretty steady groove

Death after birth after death
tenuous
as an arm. What
luck—this
music being what
initially put you in mind
Of peaceful extinction
this go round

SIMPLE TUNE

Look out for the mutilated
Who still get by OK
Yield the right of way

Straight along
The bloodied wooden rails
To a moonlit meadow
You seem to advance
In progress made of muted grays

Look out for the mutilated
Who still get by OK
Yield the right of way

SEEING THINGS AS EQUAL / BABY BULLET

Between people
    & the earth,

Nothing makes noise—
    heaven
is a relation

        Like joy—mushrooms sprouting
                out of damp earth
      in darkness

   *

The ideal basis for a comparison
will be this, your present circumstance

& your response will elide the distinctions
like listening in the car of a train, slowly

rocking along tracks in darkness
where strangers' hushed voices merge

many different languages at once
to form some single intimate sound.

   *

Dry leftover bones
saliva
bugs that make Acid Eaters

Rot Grubs
Sheep's Groom
bamboo → Green Peace Plants
Leopards
Horses
People
(Mysterious Workings)

*

Further side effects:
at a glance, the feel
motion makes
gives things sense

Sunlight on black plastic
weighted with tires over
piles of dirt. Heat, the friction
of light reflected off
eyeball to brain, simple
generation. Hello, tree. So
long. Gates swing open, brain
swings shut.

That's how useful this is—
drawing comparisons, making
distinctions

8 – 9 VI 19

CITY DIRECTORY
for Alan Bernheimer

Pinnate bright & sprouting
through cracks in gray pavement, leaves
   the sidewalk
of a chute
Not a complete thought, & buckled
by roots of trees. Footfalls
in autumn air & all the birds
flying in from somewhere
else: Mt. Tam maybe, the Palisades.
But everybody's always rushing
with their useless phyla, classification
schemes. Like you I like
speed's antonyms as they spread
spill wind out sail of head to see—
(look close & come up with) seedling
   in grate,
the little dirt in infrastructure stuff grows
in. Another word for "look close"
to come up with. Air

of several cities, on opposite coasts
of a big sleepy continent. Big bright
   canyons of light
between buildings, their tall silver sides
honking horns & movie theater marquees.
Things spelled
     as if out. Light reflected from
     high windows & down
     below sprouts
repeated lines—alleyways, a tune practiced, haltingly,
   piano from a room

overhead. Unexpected sightlines, something overheard
someone on the train said.

The city in spates
Noir slapstick,
or on great lawns of big parks
over the course of several days
conversations in record shops. It only ever
       goes on, keeps going
       for good—glancing
       up from a book
       at stops on a subway

INSCRIBED ON MY PINE STUDY

I keep a tray of paints
in a drawer in my closet study
I have few cratefuls of books
my Iranian letter opener
a SpongeBob finger board

I take it easy. No longer young
but not yet old either, I play
a little on the guitar after work.
I drink a couple of beers, sip
some hot tea. I read
'to fathom' means
to encircle w/ open arms.

Conducting these shadow studies
I have a peculiar, particularly
rapt fascination
w/ how things are spelled

I am neither here nor there—
liberal minded, mostly at ease
in my body. I have got into
         the habit
of pointing out
the case that to which
when it's pointed

disappears. Golden sneakers
& 49er headphones, a cellphone
snapshot of the moon.
The world is not

any way
anyway

& mind is a form of relation—
like the relation of rain to the ocean

SLOWNESS

Creating a slow
mausoleum, the
after-effects of
a day's work, woke
wrote as lettering
wrecked in reeds
simple to decipher as
clothes dropped on
kitchen floor
clouds, the moss
that grows on
sides of trees. Me
   & mine
is reckless
suburban nihilism
Where we say we our
cool depends
meriting signals
stars: from other
courses, outdoor
summer city rain
in strangers'
suddenly choked-up
voices. (they say the
devil's in the details
well salvation also is
& momentary but total
Surrender to them
provides a contra-
diction to nihilism)

Love not a thought
but a thinking

& always one
of many, already
different from
the thought of love

FURTHER HETERODOXY

The familiar
times & places
Of the world
are only traces—
Dreams, trance,
delusion. But
when & where I am
On the earth & of it
In granite blocks
of city streets,
on dirt roads
with wind
in trees—I
love it, it stays
in rain or sun
Truly alien
& so welcome
Outside my
mind to me

Jason Morris, 2019

Jason Morris was born and raised in Vermont. His books and chapbooks are *Spirits & Anchors* (Auguste Presse, 2010); *From the Golden West Notebooks* (Allone Co., 2011); *Local News* (Bird & Beckett, 2013); *Takes* (Bootstrap Books, 2015); *Late to Practice* (Dirty Swan Projects, 2017); and *Levon Helm* (Ugly Duckling Presse, 2018). He founded and edited the now-defunct magazine "Big Bell" from 2007 – 2014, and, along with J. Grabowski, cofounded PUSH Press.

In addition to poetry, he has written essays on Clark Coolidge's *Crystal Text*, Bernadette Mayer's interest in Nathaniel Hawthorne, and Kafka. He lives in San Francisco with his wife Sally Morris, who is a dancer.

THE PAGE POETS SERIES

Number 1
Between First & Second Sleep by Tamsin Spencer Smith

Number 2
The Michaux Notebook by Micah Ballard

Number 3
Sketch of the Artist by Patrick James Dunagan

Number 4
Different Darknesses by Jason Morris

Number 5
Suspension of Mirrors by Mary Julia Klimenko